SCHOLASTIC
ENGLISH SKILLS

Grammar and punctuation
Workbook

Ages 10–11

■SCHOLASTIC
ENGLISH SKILLS

Grammar and punctuation

Book End, Range Road, Witney, Oxfordshire, OX29 0YD
www.scholastic.co.uk

© 2015, Scholastic Ltd

6 7 8 9   8 9 0 1 2 3 4

British Library Cataloguing-in-Publication Data
A catalogue record for this book is available from the British Library.

ISBN 978-1407-14074-2
Printed in Malaysia

Author
Graham Fletcher

Editorial
Rachel Morgan, Jenny Wilcox, Red Door Media, Tracy Kewley

Design
Neil Salt, Nicolle Thomas

Cover Design
Nicolle Thomas

Illustration
Moreno Chiacchiera (Beehive Illustration)

Contents

How to use this book

- *Scholastic English Skills Workbooks* help your child to practise and improve their skills in English.

- The content is divided into topics. Find out what your child is doing in school and dip into the practice activities as required.

- Keep the working time short and come back to an activity if your child finds it too difficult. Ask your child to note any areas of difficulty. Don't worry if your child does not 'get' a concept first time, as children learn at different rates and content is likely to be covered at different times throughout the school year.

- Check your child's answers at www.scholastic.co.uk/ses/grammar.

- Give lots of encouragement, complete the 'How did you do' for each activity and the progress chart as your child finishes each chapter.

Topic
The topic you are working on.

Activity title
The title of the activity.

How did you do?
Circle Ollie Owl with a ✔ if you could do the activity. Circle Ollie Owl with a ? if you need help or more practice.

Ollie
Ollie Owl will help you with the activity.

Instruction
The instruction tells you what to do.

Activity
Follow the instruction to complete the activity.

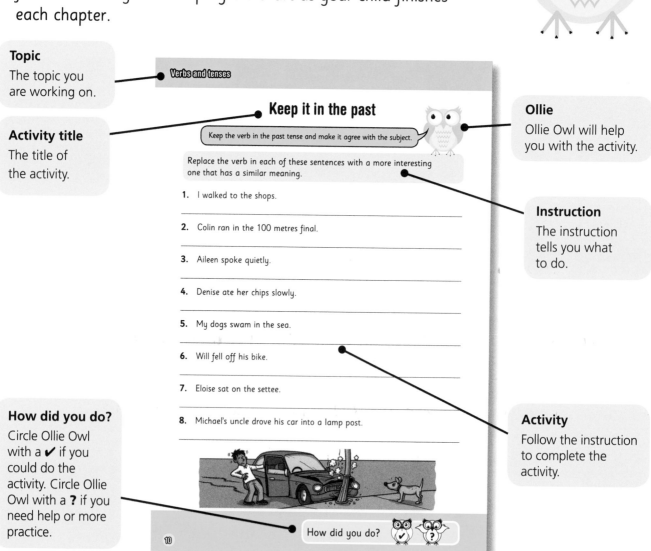

Verbs and tenses

Keep it in the past

Keep the verb in the past tense and make it agree with the subject.

Replace the verb in each of these sentences with a more interesting one that has a similar meaning.

1. I walked to the shops.
   _____

2. Colin ran in the 100 metres final.
   _____

3. Aileen spoke quietly.
   _____

4. Denise ate her chips slowly.
   _____

5. My dogs swam in the sea.
   _____

6. Will fell off his bike.
   _____

7. Eloise sat on the settee.
   _____

8. Michael's uncle drove his car into a lamp post.
   _____

How did you do?

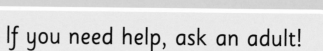

If you need help, ask an adult!

Make it agree

The subject is the person or thing that performs the verb.

The verbs and subjects in the sentences below do not agree.

Write the sentences again using the correct forms of the verbs to match the subjects.

1. Oscar and George is friends.

   Oscar and George are friends

2. Ahmed and Fisher was friends.

   Ahmed and Fish were friends

3. Alice and Kim likes music.

   Alice and Kim like Music

4. Gregory run five kilometres every day.

   Gregory ran five kilometer each day

5. There was four people in the house.

   There were four People in the house

6. We was playing football together.

   We were Playing football together

7. They hasn't brought any money with them.

   they haven't brought any money with them

8. Nathan has £1.27, I have 84p; together we has £2.11.

   Nathan has £1.27 I have we have £2.11

9. We has spent all of our money.

   We have spent all our money

10. Tom and Jane does their homework together.

    Tom and Jane do their homework together

How did you do?

5

Find the verb

Don't forget to make your subjects and verbs agree.

The passage below is written in the present tense.

Underline all of the verbs in it.

Then rewrite the passage in the past tense, underlining your new verbs.

I am in school. I am <u>writing</u> a story. In my story there are four characters. Each character is completely different:

- Ramesh is tall and has brown, wavy hair. He <u>knows</u> a lot about aeroplanes.
- Gina has blue eyes and <u>speaks</u> very clearly.
- Alex is quite small but he can <u>jump</u> very high.
- Nicola has lots of books on dinosaurs and is <u>able</u> to name most of them.

All four characters <u>go</u> to West Hill Primary School where they are in Year 6. Ramesh likes Gina and Alex but he <u>does not like</u> Nicola.

verb

I was in school. I wrote a story. In my story there were four charecters. Each charecter was comepletely dissrent. Ramesh was tall and had brown, wavy hair. He knew a lot about aeroplanes. Gina had blue eyes and spoke very clearly. Alexa was quite small but he could jump very high. Nicola had lots of books on dinosaurs and was able to name most of them. All four charecters went to west hill Primary School where in year 6 Ramesh liked Gina and alex but he did'nt like nicola

How did you do?

Mix and match

The verb must be in the correct form and the verb and subject must agree.

Look at these sentences. In each one there is a verb missing.

Use the clues in the sentences to help you choose the correct verb from the word bank to fit the space. You must only use one word of each pair.

> knows ~~knew~~   ~~competed~~ compete   arrive ~~arrived~~
> ~~ate~~ eat   end ~~began~~   go ~~went~~   bring ~~brought~~
> watch ~~watched~~   ~~finish~~ finished   complete completed

1. Yesterday I __watched__ a television programme about mice.

2. We __ate__ breakfast at 8 o'clock this morning.

3. The school holidays __finish__ next week.

4. Last Saturday I __went__ to the football with Demetri and Zak.

5. Laura __arrived__ home at 4.45pm.

6. No one __knew__ who our new class teacher will be.

7. The athlete _____ in ten events.

8. I have __completed__ my homework.

9. On Saturday we __brought__ my new dog home.

10. The holidays __finished__ a long time ago.

Choose one of your sentences and explain why you chose the verb form.

_____

_____

How did you do?

It's good to agree

Each passage below describes a situation from a different time.

Choose verbs from the boxes to fill the gaps. Change them to match the tense if necessary.

A long time ago

enjoy   live   be   see   eat   share   go   have   make

My mother _____ born in the 1980s. Her family _*lived*_ in a semi-detached house. My mother _*had*_ her own bedroom, unlike her two brothers who _*shared*_ one. They all _____ to Mount Road Primary, which they _*enjoyed*_ going to. At lunchtime they _*ate*_ sandwiches. They all _*made*_ some good friends at school and still _*See*_ some of them today.

Today

have   give   choose   live   wake up   sleep   buy   catch   work

I _____ in a multi-storey building. It _____ 17 floors and the lift often doesn't _____. It is hard to _____ because of the traffic noise, so I often _____ tired. My mum _____ me money for my bus fare to school and I _____ how to spend it. Sometimes I _____ sweets with it and hope I don't get _____ eating them in class!

How did you do?

When is it happening?

In each sentence below, underline the words that tell you whether the sentence is talking about the present, the past or the future.

Write the time in the space next to each sentence. The first one has been done for you.

1. I <u>am going</u> to play on my games console. _____future_____

2. I can't get the internet to work. _____Present_____

3. It's Monday. _____Present_____

4. I went to school. _____Past_____

5. I will be going to a new school in September. _____Future_____

6. It is cold today. _____Present_____

7. The weather last Friday was awful. _____Past_____

8. The weather tomorrow will be good. _____Future_____

9. I will do some online shopping on Saturday. _____Future_____

10. I'm happy. _____Present_____

How did you do?

Keep it in the past

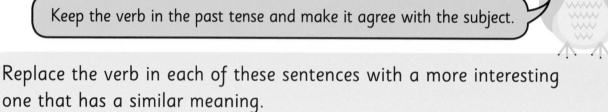

Keep the verb in the past tense and make it agree with the subject.

Replace the verb in each of these sentences with a more interesting one that has a similar meaning.

1. I walked to the shops.

_____

2. Colin ran in the 100 metres final.

_____

3. Aileen spoke quietly.

_____

4. Denise ate her chips slowly.

_____

5. My dogs swam in the sea.

_____

6. Will fell off his bike.

_____

7. Eloise sat on the settee.

_____

8. Michael's uncle drove his car into a lamp post.

_____

How did you do?

Irregular verbs

To make the past form of a verb we can usually add 'ed' to the end of the present form. For example: **watch** becomes **watched**. Irregular verbs don't follow this rule however.

Write the past form of each of these irregular verbs in the spaces below.

1. begin _Began_

2. bring _brought_

3. buy _bought_

4. catch _caught_

5. creep _crept_

6. do _did_

7. draw _drew_

8. eat _ate_

9. fall _fell_

10. fly _flew_

11. give _gave_

12. hold _held_

13. leave _left_

14. meet _met_

15. take _took_

How did you do?

Present perfect

The present perfect form uses 'have' or 'has' and another verb.

Tick the boxes of the sentences that use the present perfect form of verbs. Leave the boxes empty for those sentences that do not.

1. I went to Belgium on a ferry. ☐
2. I have been to Belgium. ☑
3. I had been to Belgium. ☐
4. The choir has performed lots of songs. ☑
5. I did a sponsored walk for charity. ☐
6. Toby has done a sponsored walk for charity. ☑
7. Jill and Mary have been away for a week. ☑
8. Jill and Mary went away for a week. ☑
9. No one has seen the missing treasure. ☑
10. Corey and Will have twenty pounds each. ☐

Pick two of your answers. Use the boxes below to explain why you think one is in the present perfect form and one is not.

Sentence number _____ **is** in the present perfect form because
_____.

Sentence number _____ **is not** in the present perfect form because
_____.

How did you do?

Past perfect

The following sentence is in the past perfect form:
Ronnie **had won** the race.

Tick the boxes of the sentences that use the past perfect form of verbs. Leave the boxes empty for those sentences that do not.

1. I had walked to the chip shop. ❏

2. I have eaten chips for tea. ❏

3. I downloaded an MP3 file. ❏

4. I had used the internet to research for my history project. ❏

5. I had bought a new dress. ❏

6. Louis has been off school all week. ❏

7. Celia's phone has stopped working. ❏

8. Pat had finished his meal. ❏

9. My cat has come home. ❏

10. Sharon had lost her purse. ❏

Pick two of your answers. Use the boxes below to explain why you think one is in the past perfect form and one is not.

Sentence number _____ **is** in the past perfect form because

_____.

Sentence number _____ **is not** in the past perfect form because

_____.

How did you do?

Present perfect versus past perfect

Write an appropriate verb to fill the gaps in the following sentences.

Use clues in the sentences to help you to decide whether to use the past perfect or the present perfect form.

For each sentence, explain why you have chosen the form you have.

1. I _____ toast for breakfast for a whole year.

_____

_____

2. I had beans and sausages for tea yesterday even though

I _____ beans on toast for lunch.

_____

_____

3. We _____ to Marbella for two weeks every summer.

_____

_____

4. My mother _____ bingo on Saturdays for as long as I can remember.

_____

_____

5. I _____ in goal until I broke my leg.

_____

_____

How did you do?

Simple to perfect

The following sentences are all written in the simple present form.
Rewrite them so that they are in the past perfect form.

For example: I carry the shopping home. = I had carried the shopping home.

1. Billy sees his friends.

_____

2. Sara ate breakfast.

_____

3. Lester rides a motorbike.

_____

The following sentences are all written in the simple present form.
Rewrite them so that they are in the present perfect form.

For example: I play in the park. = I have played in the park.

4. I look at lots of maps in geography at school.

_____

5. Stuart plays guitar every day.

_____

6. Cara feeds her cat regularly.

_____

7. Josef and Gretel visit their grandmother each Thursday.

_____

How did you do?

Who is the strongest?

Modal verbs work with other verbs to tell you about their condition or likelihood.

All of the modal verbs are in the boxes on the right-hand side of the page. Write them in the correct places on the Test Your Strength machine. Put the weakest at the bottom and the strongest at the top.

will   ought   shall

might   should   must   may

could   can   would

1.

2.

3.

4.

5.

6.

7.

8.

9.

10.

How did you do?

Is it likely?

Tick the box next to the sentence you think is most likely to happen. Give a reason for your choice.

I ought to go to see Julie now. ☐

I will go to see Julie now. ☐

I might go to see Julie now. ☐

Reason: _____

Tick the box next to the sentence you think is least likely to happen. Give a reason for your choice.

I could go to see Julie now. ☐

I shall go to see Julie now. ☐

I must go to see Julie now. ☐

Reason: _____

Make up three similar sentences using modal verbs. Write the most likely at the top and the least likely at the bottom.

	Most likely
	↑ ↓
	Least likely

How did you do?

Is there a choice?

The modal verbs in the sentences below show that it is probable that the events will happen.

Rewrite them using different modal verbs so that they are only possible. Use a different modal verb for each sentence.

1. I ought to help with the washing up.

   _____

2. I shall take the dog for a walk.

   _____

3. I must eat fewer sweets.

   _____

Make up three similar sentences using modal verbs that show events that are only possible. Use a different modal verb in each sentence.

_____

_____

_____

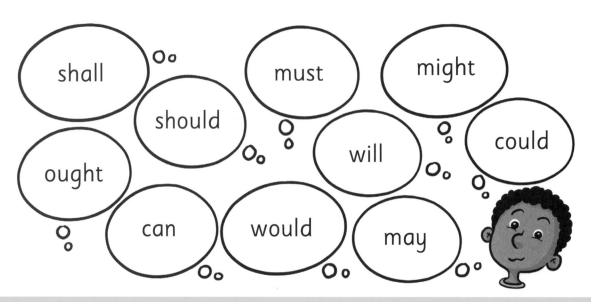

How did you do?

Are you likely to do it not?

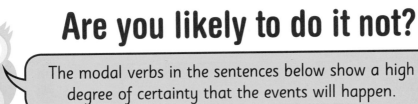

The modal verbs in the sentences below show a high degree of certainty that the events will happen.

Rewrite them using different modal verbs so that they are only probable. Use a different modal verb for each sentence.

1. I will pay back the money that I owe you.

_____

2. I can lend you some money.

_____

3. I shall give you some money for your birthday.

_____

4. I will stop lending you money.

_____

Now make up four similar sentences that show events that are probable. Use a different modal verb in each sentence.

_____

_____

_____

_____

Probable: must, would, should, ought.

How did you do?

19

Match the synonym

Synonyms are words with similar meanings.

Complete the diagrams below by adding the correct synonyms from the list at the bottom of the page. You will have four words left.

big

happy

little

sad

annoyed	small	outraged	petite	gloomy
enormous	cheerful	tiny	pleased	ecstatic
delighted	diminutive	colossal	depressed	furious
cheerless	miserable	huge	livid	gigantic

List the four words you have not used and write one synonym that will apply to all of them.

Four words: _____

My synonym: _____

How did you do?

Swap the synonyms

Synonym means similar.

Replace the bold words in each of the following sentences with a synonym so that the meaning of each sentence remains the same.

1. All Formula 1 cars move **quickly**.

    _____

2. I decided to **throw out** all of the toys I no longer used.

    _____

3. I wouldn't have made it on time if I hadn't **eaten** my breakfast quickly.

    _____

4. When I looked down from the top of the building I was **scared**.

    _____

5. I had plenty of time so I **walked** slowly to school.

    _____

6. I was late so I had to **run** to school.

    _____

7. There was a terrible **smell** coming from the toilets!

    _____

8. I thought the maths test was really **simple**.

    _____

9. The sun **shone** brightly every day during my holiday in Greece.

    _____

10. It was that **funny**, I fell off my chair laughing.

    _____

How did you do?

Circle the synonyms

Circle all of the words in each list that are synonyms for the word in bold in the sentence.

1. Yesterday was a **nice** day.

   horrible   pleasant   dreadful   good   lovely   terrible   enjoyable

2. My cat was **wet** when it came in from the rain.

   soaked   dry   drenched   waterless   parched   soggy   dripping

3. Stroking a crocodile is **dangerous**!

   safe   risky   perilous   unsafe   harmless   hazardous

4. It is **sensible** to look for traffic before you cross the road.

   stupid   reasonable   foolish   sane   wise   silly   unwise   prudent

5. My favourite meal is a **delicious** curry.

   scrumptious   tasty   flavourless   delectable   bland   yummy   tasteless

Now look at the words you have not circled. See how they relate to the underlined words in the sentences.

What is the name we give to words like these? _____

How did you do?

Synonyms and antonyms

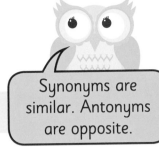

Synonyms are similar. Antonyms are opposite.

Replace the bold word in each sentence with a synonym.

1. Blackpool Tower is a very **tall** building.

_____

2. Millionaires are very **rich** people.

_____

3. I think purple is a **horrible** colour.

_____

4. Giving money to charity is a **good** thing to do.

_____

5. University lecturers are **clever** people.

_____

Replace the underlined word in each sentence with an antonym.

6. I think purple is a **horrible** colour.

_____

7. Very few people are **honest**.

_____

8. I think running is a **wonderful** sport.

_____

9. I **never** eat unhealthy foods.

_____

10. The crowd at the football match was very **quiet**.

_____

How did you do?

Which would you use?

In the boxes below, write whether you would use formal or informal language for the situation described.

Giving evidence in court
_____

A set of notes
_____

A contract for a job
_____

A news report
_____

Telephoning your sister
_____

Email to a friend
_____

An application for a job
_____

A shopping list
_____

A talk in assembly for Year 6 children
_____

Leaving an answerphone message for your mum
_____

Choose one formal and one informal situation from the boxes above and write an opening sentence for it.

Formal: _____

Informal: _____

How did you do?

They use both!

All the situations below need both formal and informal language at different times.

In the boxes, give examples of who might use the different forms of language and when.

Situation 1: In school

formal	informal

Situation 2: On television

formal	informal

Situation 3: In newspapers

formal	informal

How did you do?

Formal and informal

Sometimes formal and informal language can be used at the same time. For example, your teacher may ask you a question using formal language but you might reply using informal language.

In the boxes below, write an interview between a television presenter and the eyewitness of a bank robbery. The interviewer must speak using formal language throughout but the eyewitness can use a mixture of formal and informal language.

Interviewer	
Eyewitness	
Interviewer	
Eyewitness	
Interviewer	
Eyewitness	

Explain why you think the interviewer would use formal language.

_____

_____

How did you do?

Match the meanings

Draw lines to connect the sentences that have similar meanings.

Decide which you think are formal and write 'Formal' in the boxes containing those sentences.

You what?

_____

There are large numbers of children in the park today

_____

To summarise, the solution is obvious.

_____

You're getting on my nerves.

_____

I haven't seen you for some time.

_____

Pardon?

_____

You are annoying me.

_____

In a nutshell, the answer's right there, under your nose.

_____

There's tons of kids in the park today.

_____

That will not be difficult.

_____

No probs. I can do that easily.

_____

Long time, no see.

_____

How did you do?

Which would you use?

Next to each of the following statements, write whether they use formal or informal language.

1. It would be really helpful if you could... _____

2. Can you give us a hand? _____

3. Any idea where the railway station is? _____

4. Can you direct me to the railway station, please? _____

5. This really is quite fantastic. _____

6. Wowzer! _____

7. Good on you, pal! _____

8. Congratulations, that is an excellent result. _____

Next to each of the following situations, write whether you should use formal or informal language in them.

9. Telephoning a doctor's surgery to make an appointment. _____

10. Meeting a friend. _____

11. A parent calling the school to report a child's illness. _____

12. Accepting a job offer. _____

13. Talking to your parents. _____

14. Speaking at a school council meeting. _____

15. Complaining about something you have bought. _____

How did you do?

Car crash or collision?

René Porter needs to write a newspaper report on a car crash. Unfortunately, the witness's statement is full of informal language.

Read the witness statement. Then rewrite it using formal language as a report for the newspaper.

"Well, I was walking down the street, minding my own business when I heard the screeching of tyres. So I looks to my left and I sees a car belting down the middle of High Street. He was going a fair whack. He was pushing 100mph I'd say, but the woman next to me said it were nowt like that. Still, the car swerved towards the kerb and all the people had to leg it out of the way. It was proper dangerous, like. There were loads of kids and mums there. Luckily, it missed them all. It gave the lamp post a bit of a whack and then bounced off like a ping-pong ball to the wall at the far end of the street. That was it. I was straight on my mobile. I called the police, the ambulance and the fire people. I even called the RSPCA. It was a stroke of luck that nobody was hurt."

How did you do?

Formal to informal

Fill in the gaps with formal or informal versions of the phrases below.

Formal	Informal
Letter: Dear Kerry,	**Email**:
Phone call: I will see you at 8 o'clock.	**Text**:
Newspaper report:	**Eyewitness report**: I heard shedloads of big bangs at the power station.
Autobiography: The sun shone brightly. I knew today would be a fabulous day.	**Diary**:

The following text explains how to make a cup of tea using formal language. Rewrite using informal language.

There is a very clear process involved in making the perfect cup of tea. Start by boiling enough water for the amount of people who will be drinking. Then put one teabag per person into a cup. When the water has boiled, pour it gently over the teabag. Stir the teabag then press it against the side of the cup. Remove the tea bag carefully, taking care not to spill the tea. Next, add milk or sugar to your taste. Finally, sit back and enjoy your tea.

_____

_____

_____

_____

How did you do?

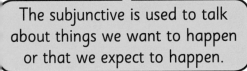

The subjunctive is used to talk about things we want to happen or that we expect to happen.

Subjunctive

Choose the subjunctive form of the verbs to complete each sentence.

1. I insist that everybody _____ carefully.	listen, listens, listened
2. The School Council proposes that we _____ early on Fridays.	finished, finishes, finish
3. The team manager demands that we _____ on time.	are, be
4. I wish I _____ on holiday today.	was, were
5. The Police advise that motorists _____ carefully in bad weather.	drove, drive, driven
6. I insist that Ella _____ invited to my party.	be, is, was
7. The doctor recommended that her patient _____ in hospital.	remain, remains, remained
8. Head teachers recommend that more money _____ invested in schools.	be, is
9. Experts suggest that children _____ fewer video games.	play, plays, played
10. The interviewer asked that the prime minister _____ something about schools.	said, says, say

How did you do?

Phrases followed by the subjunctive

Choose the subjunctive form of the verbs to complete each sentence.

1. It is very important that all children going on the trip _____ ready for 8 o'clock.	are, be
2. It is essential that water _____ preserved in dry weather.	is, be, was
3. It is a good idea that people _____ money to charity.	give, gave, given
4. It is recommended that you _____ a helmet when cycling.	wore, wear
5. It is crucial that you _____ there before the bus arrives.	are, be
6. It is vital that children _____ hard preparing for exams.	work, worked
7. It is desirable that debt _____ avoided.	is, be
8. It is a bad idea that we _____ out in the rain without an umbrella.	goes, go
9. It is urgent that we _____ food to starving children.	sent, send
10. It is imperative that the team manager _____ immediately.	resigns, resign

How did you do?

You want to get these right, don't you?

Add an appropriate question tag from the boxes below to these statements.

Make the verbs and the pronouns in the question tags agree with the verbs and the subjects in the statements.

1. You don't like dancing, _____?

2. You won't do that again, _____?

3. You've not been to London, _____?

4. We won't be going to the cinema on Saturday, _____?

5. You couldn't help me carry this, _____?

6. Ice skating can be quite dangerous, _____?

7. You need to take care crossing the road, _____?

8. Old people are entitled to respect, _____?

9. People shouldn't drop litter, _____?

10. There's too much football on television, _____?

can't it	have you	will we	don't you	will you
could you	isn't there	aren't they	do you	should they

You'd like to do these, wouldn't you?

Verbs and pronouns must agree throughout the sentence.

Add an appropriate question tag to the following statements.

1. You haven't finished your meal, _____?

2. You aren't thinking of going out in that, _____?

3. We don't want to go there again, _____?

4. I couldn't ask you for a loan, _____?

5. People don't waterski in deserts, _____?

6. That's not a clever thing to do, _____?

7. The roads are always very busy on bank holidays, _____?

8. There's no need to shout, _____?

9. Your uncle is arriving on Sunday, _____?

10. Your grandparents won't like your music much, _____?

How did you do?

Identify the subject and the object

Circle the **subject** in the sentences below.

1. I have lost my mobile phone.

2. Demi rode her horse.

3. The dog ate its food.

4. The sun shone all day.

5. The lion roared at the hunters.

Subject = does it.

Choose one of the sentences above and explain why the word you have chosen is the subject.

_____

_____

Circle the **object** in the following sentences.

6. The postman delivered the letters.

7. Eliza polished her fingernails.

8. The orchestra played the symphony.

9. Millions of people watched the Olympics.

10. Roger has broken his games console.

Object = has it done.

Choose one of the sentences above and explain why the word you have chosen is the object.

_____

_____

How did you do?

Subjects, objects and verbs

Write the subjects, objects and verbs under each sentence below.

1. Rhonda looked in her mirror.

Subject: _____ Object: _____ Verb: _____

2. Asif crashed his car.

Subject: _____ Object: _____ Verb: _____

3. Caroline lost her bracelet.

Subject: _____ Object: _____ Verb: _____

4. Otis bought six plums.

Subject: _____ Object: _____ Verb: _____

5. Shana wore her new trainers.

Subject: _____ Object: _____ Verb: _____

6. Rudi ate a bag of crisps.

Subject: _____ Object: _____ Verb: _____

7. Jaz kicked his football.

Subject: _____ Object: _____ Verb: _____

8. Tiff visited her cousin.

Subject: _____ Object: _____ Verb: _____

9. Beth watched the television.

Subject: _____ Object: _____ Verb: _____

How did you do?

Who is doing what?

For each of these sentences, circle the **subject** and tick whether it is doing something or having something done to it.

1. The dog chased the postman.
    Doing something ☐   Having something done to it ☐

2. The postman was chased by the dog.
    Doing something ☐   Having something done to it ☐

3. The farmer ploughed the field.
    Doing something ☐   Having something done to it ☐

4. The field was ploughed by the farmer.
    Doing something ☐   Having something done to it ☐

5. The cup was won by the school team.
    Doing something ☐   Having something done to it ☐

6. The school team won the cup.
    Doing something ☐   Having something done to it ☐

7. Rita was invited to Abigail's party.
    Doing something ☐   Having something done to it ☐

8. Abigail invited Rita to her party.
    Doing something ☐   Having something done to it ☐

9. A celebrity switched on the illuminations.
    Doing something ☐   Having something done to it ☐

10. The illuminations were switched on by a celebrity.
    Doing something ☐   Having something done to it ☐

How did you do?

Changing the subject

Rewrite each of these sentences so that the object becomes the subject. The first one has been done for you.

For example: The cat sat on the mat. _The mat was sat on by the cat_

1. Katie drank a litre of milk.

   _____

2. Felix caught a burglar.

   _____

3. Heavy rain flooded the streets.

   _____

4. A power cut turned all of the lights out.

   _____

5. JK Rowling wrote the _Harry Potter_ books.

   _____

6. William the Conqueror won the Battle of Hastings.

   _____

7. The Queen awarded medals for bravery.

   _____

8. The bank robbers used a getaway car.

   _____

9. A volcanic eruption destroyed Pompeii.

   _____

How did you do?

Another past

In an active sentence the subject performs the verb and the object receives it.

The verbs in the following sentences have been put in bold.

Circle if you think they are active or passive.

In a passive sentence the order is reversed so the object is doing the action.

1. My family **went** on holiday.   Active   Passive

2. The plane **was flown** by the pilot.   Active   Passive

3. They **collected** their belongings.   Active   Passive

4. My sister's bag **was stolen** by a thief.   Active   Passive

5. The police **arrived** very quickly.   Active   Passive

6. The purse **was found** by a cleaner.   Active   Passive

7. It **had been** emptied.   Active   Passive

8. Her passport **had disappeared**.   Active   Passive

9. The police **called** the British Consulate.   Active   Passive

10. A new passport **was issued** to her.   Active   Passive

How did you do?

Make it passive

Complete each sentence with the passive form of the verb that is in brackets. Use **is** or **are** as the helping verb. The first one has been done for you.

For example: The television (watch) <u>is watched</u> by Sophie.

1. The meal (serve) _____ by waiters.

2. The medicine (take) _____ by the patient.

3. The horse (ride) _____ by a jockey.

4. Letters (deliver) _____ by the postman.

5. Newspapers (write) _____ by journalists.

Complete each sentence in the passive form but this time use the past form of the helping verb. The first one has been done for you.

For example: Everyone (tell) <u>was told</u> about the school trip.

6. My new trainers (buy) _____ by my mum.

7. Our car (repair) _____ by a mechanic.

8. Our meal (make) _____ by a really good chef.

9. The Mona Lisa (paint) _____ by Leonardo da Vinci.

10. The work (finish) _____ by the end of the day.

Was is the past form of **is**. **Were** is the past form of **are**.

How did you do? ✔ ?

Find the passive verbs

Read the follow piece of writing and circle each of the verbs that is used in the passive voice.

Millions of years ago, the world was inhabited by dinosaurs. Many smaller creatures were attacked and eaten by them. However, not all dinosaurs were dangerous. Usually, dinosaurs are shown in films as flesh-eating monsters but many only ate plants. Large numbers of trees and shrubs were eaten daily. Evidence of dinosaurs is found all over the world but no living dinosaurs have been discovered.

Read the passage again and find a clause that can be written using an active verb. Rewrite it in the space below.

_____

Why do you think so many of the verbs in the text are in the passive voice?

_____
_____
_____
_____
_____
_____

How did you do?

From active to passive

All of the sentences below are written in the active voice. Rewrite them in the passive.

1. The pirate counted the treasure.

_____

2. The wizard practised two new spells.

_____

3. Four boys sailed model boats.

_____

4. Gemma and Martha held an online video conference.

_____

5. The head teacher wrote a letter to the parents.

_____

6. Sal ordered fish and chips.

_____

7. The taxi brought my aunt from the station to our house.

_____

8. John Logie Baird gave the first public demonstration of televised images in 1925.

_____

9. The Duke of Wellington's army won the Battle of Waterloo.

_____

10. The storm battered the pier at Southend.

_____

How did you do?

From passive to active

All of the sentences below are written in the passive voice. Rewrite them in the active.

1. *Treasure Island* was written by Robert Louis Stevenson.

    _____

2. The role of the Mad Hatter in *Alice in Wonderland* was played by Johnny Depp.

    _____

3. Mount Everest was first climbed by Sir Edmund Hillary.

    _____

4. In 2014, the FIFA World Cup was won by Germany.

    _____

5. St Paul's Cathedral was designed by Sir Christopher Wren.

    _____

6. Much of London was destroyed in the Great Fire of 1666.

    _____

7. South East England was struck by a hurricane in 1987.

    _____

8. The English Channel was first flown across by Louis Blériot.

    _____

9. Traffic is being held up by an accident on the M25 again.

    _____

10. Over a hundred medals were won by British athletes at the 2012 Paralympic Games.

    _____

How did you do?

Using the passive voice

For each of the verbs below, write a sentence using the passive voice. The first one has been done for you.

Example: Verb: **take** Sentence: _The parcel was taken to the post office._

1. Verb: **send** Sentence: _____

   _____

2. Verb: **carry** Sentence: _____

   _____

3. Verb: **build** Sentence: _____

   _____

4. Verb: **run** Sentence: _____

   _____

5. Verb: **write** Sentence: _____

   _____

6. Verb: **read** Sentence: _____

   _____

7. Verb: **listen** Sentence: _____

   _____

8. Verb: **fly** Sentence: _____

   _____

9. Verb: **ate** Sentence: _____

   _____

How did you do?

Your passive and active voice story

Write a passage of text including both active and passive verbs.

Underline your passive verbs and circle your active verbs.

Use the pictures to help you and make sure you have at least one sentence for each picture.

How did you do?

A clause for thought

Clauses are useful for improving your writing. Each sentence has a main clause containing a subject and a verb.

Circle the subject in the following sentences.

1. Josef is going home.

2. The holidays are over.

3. Greece is a hot country.

4. The city airport closes at midnight.

The sentences below all have two clauses. One is the **main clause**, the other is a **relative clause**. The relative clause is a subordinate clause that tells us more about the main clause.

Underline the main clauses and circle the relative clauses in these sentences.

5. I went to Trinidad, which is in the Caribbean Sea.

6. I gave some sweets to Bilal, who enjoyed them.

7. I walked to the bus stop, which is at the end of the street.

8. My cousin, who is very rich, lives in Kingston upon Thames.

How is number 8 different from the other three examples?

_____

_____

_____

_____

How did you do?

Find the clause

Circle the main clauses in the sentences below.

1. I like ice skating because I take part in competitions.

2. Tomorrow the weather will be good though it will rain on Tuesday.

3. Jim travels to work by bus even though he had a car.

4. Charlotte was born in France whereas her mother was born in England.

Circle the subordinate clauses in the sentences below.

5. I am going to Glastonbury Festival this year although I can't go next year.

6. I am good at maths because I like numbers.

7. I am going to buy a new skirt before I get the bus home.

Circle the conjunctions that link the clauses in these sentences.

8. Jerry was sent home from school because he was unwell.

9. The umpire was usually good but he made some bad decisions today.

10. We went to the zoo where we saw some penguins.

How did you do?

Add a clause

Extend the sentences by adding a relative clause.

1. Aneka hit the ball _____

2. Christopher approached the castle's gates _____

3. Sonia raced up the aircraft steps _____

4. Andrea tried on some new shoes _____

5. My parents were born in Jamaica _____

Extend the sentences by adding a subordinate clause.

6. The meal was served _____

7. Three prisoners were locked up _____

8. My broken radio was repaired _____

9. A new 100 metres world record was set _____

10. Alex was taken to dance lessons _____

How did you do?

Match the clauses

Draw arrows to link the main clauses on the left of the page with the correct subordinate clauses on the right of the page.

Main

Subordinate

Roger played outside in the garden

which is the country with the largest population in the world.

Robert Scott reached the South Pole

that are over a hundred years old.

The children went to bed

when I started primary school.

I've always liked Natalie

after he wrote *The BFG*.

My gran has some photographs

until his mum called to say dinner was ready.

My elder sister started secondary school

though Roald Amundsen had got there first.

Chloe and Rosie are twins

whereas subordinate ones don't.

Matilda was written by Roald Dahl

because she is kind.

My cousin lives in China

although they are not identical.

Main clauses make sense by themselves

after they had cleaned their teeth.

How did you do?

Make the link

Write the words and phrases in the correct places in the table.

Cohesive device	Examples
Adverbials of manner	
Adverbials of place	
Adverbials of time	
Adverbs	
Conjunctions	
Determiners	
Pronouns	

in the corner   as soon as she was ready   meanwhile

at the health centre   with great skill   four   next Friday

at night   roughly   she   an   he   but   my

How did you do?

Link the clauses

and, **but**, **for**, **nor**, **or**, **so**, and **yet** are coordinating conjunctions.

Link the following independent clauses by using coordinating conjunctions.

1. I like playing tennis _____ I am not very good at it.

2. My sister gets the bus to town _____ she doesn't have to walk.

3. I have lots of friends _____ I like them all equally.

4. My cousin might come to see me on Saturday _____ she might come on Sunday instead.

5. I didn't get in the team _____ I hadn't practised enough.

Complete the sentences by using subordinating conjunctions.

6. I bought the dress _____ of the colour.

7. We had maths and PE _____ lunch.

8. I've been able to swim _____ last year.

9. Big elephants eat more food _____ smaller elephants.

10. This is the house _____ Shakespeare used to live.

after, **although**, **as**, **because**, **if**, **since**, **than**, **that**, **though**, **when**, **where** and **while** are examples of subordinating conjunctions, but there are others.

How did you do?

Make cohesive links

Each piece of writing below contains the end of one paragraph and the start of the next.

Use a cohesive device to write the missing sentence for the second paragraph.

Write the name of each device you have used in the boxes. You can only use each device once.

1. Aarti was horrified as she watched the door slam behind her. _____

_____

She was locked out!

Cohesive device used: _____

2. Aarti sat on the doorstep and thought hard.

_____

_____

She decided to call her mother

Cohesive device used: _____

3. Her mother laughed when she was told but she said she would be back soon.

_____

_____ Aarti grabbed the key, unlocked the door and ran inside.

Cohesive device used: _____

How did you do?

Using synonyms to help cohesion

In each of the passages below, replace the words in bold with synonyms to give the text more cohesion and avoid repetition.

Rudi opened his book and began to read. **The book** _____ was an imaginative story about the time when dinosaurs ruled the Earth. **The story** _____ gave lots of interesting details about **dinosaurs** _____. **Rudi** _____ knew that not all of **the details** _____ were true. **The details** _____ couldn't all be **true** _____ because it was **an imaginative story** _____.

Snow fell heavily, blowing great drifts against the windows of Scarlet's house. Inside **the house** _____, Scarlet felt safe and warm. She looked out of **the window** _____ and **looked** _____ at **the great drifts** _____ that blocked her view of the street. **In the street** _____, a boy and a girl were playing, throwing snowballs at each other. Scarlet wanted to join **the boy and the girl** _____ but she also **wanted** _____ to stay **inside** _____ where it was **warm** _____.

Trudy was very angry. **Trudy was angry** _____ because her sister, Millie, had borrowed her bike again. **Millie** _____ never asked permission. **Millie** _____ just took the bike whenever she felt like it. Trudy had told **Millie** _____ that if she took the bike again without **permission** _____, there would be trouble.

How did you do?

Ellipsis

Ellipsis is when expected or predictable words are missed out.

In the replies to the questions below, underline the words that are not needed and could be missed out.

	Question	Reply
1.	"Can you tell me the time?"	"Yes, it's four o'clock."
2.	"What is four times four?"	"It is sixteen."
3.	"What is your favourite city?"	"My favourite city is New York."
4.	"Where are you going?"	"I am going to the shop."
5.	"Who won the Battle of Hastings?"	"William the Conqueror won it."

Try to work out the words that are missing from the following sentences and write them in the gaps. Remember, they should be predictable.

6. My sister went ice skating I couldn't _____.

7. "Do you know the way to the school office?"

    "Yes _____"

8. "Is it quicker for you to walk to school or to use the bus?"

    "_____ to walk."

9. "How tall are you?" "_____146cm."

10. "How many sisters do you have?"

    "_____ four _____."

How did you do?

Tidy it up

Underline the words that are not needed and could be missed out in the sentences below.

The sentences still need to make sense.

1. You can choose whichever clothes you want to wear.

2. There were lot of rides and lots of stalls at the fair.

3. Hugo finished his book and then went out to play.

4. I wore my new top, my new jeans and my new shoes at the dance.

5. Darcey didn't want to do her homework but her mum said she had to do it.

Underline the words that have been repeated in the sentences below. Then join the sentences together to make one sentence. The first one has been done for you.

For example: <u>Jed</u> has a new games console.
<u>Jed</u> uses his games console to play his latest games.

<u>Jed has a new games console that he uses to play his latest games.</u>

6. Mia and Lily love to sing. Mia and Lily sing in a choir on Tuesday nights.

_____

7. Jo is good at chess. Jo practises chess every night.

_____

8. My cousin has a beautiful kitten. My cousin's kitten is ginger and white. The kitten is very cute.

_____

How did you do?

55

Write your own clues

Lola has to organise a treasure hunt. Here is her first clue.

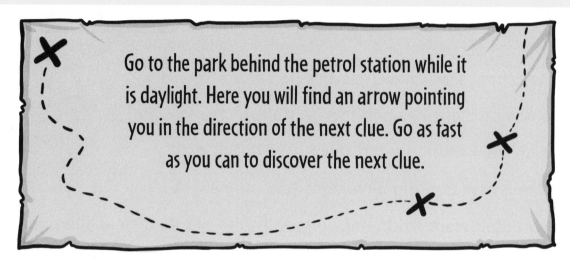

Go to the park behind the petrol station while it is daylight. Here you will find an arrow pointing you in the direction of the next clue. Go as fast as you can to discover the next clue.

Use at least one adverbial from each of the boxes below to help you write the next clue.

Adverbials of time	Adverbials of manner	Adverbials of place
As soon as possible	With great effort	At the end of the street
A little later	At lightning pace	In front of the supermarket
By the end of the week	With no trouble at all	Under the arches

_____

_____

_____

_____

_____

How did you do?

Headline writer

Keep to the point.

Below is a summary of the information in three different articles. Write a headline for each article.

Headline: _____

- Three boys in your school have chickenpox.
- They have been told not to come into school.
- Other parents are worried.
- The local health centre is very busy.

Headline: _____

- There has been terrible weather in the south of the country.
- Heavy rain has fallen for two days.
- Many of the towns have been flooded.
- Hundreds of people have had to leave their homes.

Headline: _____

- A company is offering holidays to Mars.
- They will cost £275,000 each.
- No one has been there before.
- Some experts say that the trip is not safe.

How did you do?

Headings and subheadings

Be original but brief!

The article below is from a holiday brochure. Read it and then add an appropriate headings and subheadings in the boxes.

Heading: _____

Subheading: _____

Zadar. Where? It's not surprising you don't know. Zadar is a small town on the coast of Croatia. It's a little-known gem that has only just been discovered by British holidaymakers.

Subheading: _____

What is there to do there? Almost nothing. If you want beaches, this isn't the place for you but if you like eating and drinking in fabulous restaurants serving local food at really cheap prices then this is the place for you!

Subheading: _____

If you like scenery, the Plitvice Lakes National Park is only a short drive away. Here you will find the most fabulous series of waterfalls that you could ever imagine. If you are feeling adventurous and energetic, Paklenica National Park, an even shorter distance up the coast, is a climber's playground.

Subheading: _____

Zadar is an old town with bags of charm and atmosphere. But it's not easy to get to. Only budget airlines fly there at present. This is your chance to get in before the crowds!

How did you do?

What's important?

Read the information about three different products below.

Make a bullet pointed list of the important things about each product in the spaces.

SCORCHER

Scorcher stickers help you play better.

The cutting edge technology gives you more control of the ball. Micropores help the ball stick to your foot. With these on your boots, you won't just score, you'll SCOR-CHER!

AVAILABLE IN MOST SUPERMARKETS

Scorcher:

_____

_____

_____

_____

The GOOD GUIDE

A new local magazine that tells you what's on in your area every month.

It is aimed at 10–12 year olds. You'll find info on where to go and what to do.

£2.50 PER MONTH

FROM ALL GOOD NEWSAGENTS

The Good Guide:

_____

_____

_____

_____

 **SwimFin**

A fantastic new idea. If you can't swim, strap on a fin – that's what fish do!

Made of high-tech, low-cost, long-lasting plastic, the Swim Fin is ideal if you are not confident in the water. Take it on holiday with you and strut your watery stuff!

Swim Fin:

_____

_____

_____

_____

How did you do?

Summarising with bullet points

Read the information below. Then rewrite it as a list using bullet points.

CLEANITALL

World-leading washing powder manufacturers, Cleanitall, have made a new washing powder called All White that is 20% more effective at getting rid of stains than their previous products. All White uses 'Bright' technology to give the cleanest wash ever. It can be used on the lowest temperatures. All White is available in all good shops.

COLDCURE

Professor Rachel Hankins has discovered a cure for the common cold. She has worked for ten years on the project. Millions of people will feel the benefit of it but it will not be available in the shops for another five years. Professor Hankins is likely to receive a Nobel Prize for her work.

How did you do?

Which would you choose?

Write two different sentences about your school.

_____

_____

We use layout devices to structure our writing so readers can easily understand it.

Now present your information as a table.

Present it as a magazine article in columns with headings and subheadings.

Which of the two layouts do you think works better?

I think the better one is _____ because _____

_____

_____

How did you do?

Abel's table

Abel has been asked to collect information about some people in his class for the school newsletter. He has put it into a table.

Name	Hair colour	Height	Hobbies	Dislikes	Favourite subject
Alicia	blonde	136cm	riding horses, listening to music	rude people	PE
Franz	black	152cm	collecting postcards	Monday mornings	science
Owen	light brown	146cm	writing stories	video games	English
Rashid	black	149cm	drawing and painting	getting up early	art

Write an article based on the information Abel has collected. You need to write it in columns but how will you organise it?

■ With a section on each person?

■ By topic?

■ Another way?

Include a title for your writing, headings for each column and subheadings if necessary. Will you include pictures? If you do, which columns will you put them in?

Plan your piece on a separate piece of paper then write neatly on the next page.

How did you do?

Title	
Heading	Heading
Heading	Heading

How did you do?

Timetable

Use the table below to make the following information easier to read.

On **Mondays**, Willow Class will have English, maths, history, geography and PE. On **Tuesdays** they will have English, maths, Spanish, music and art. On **Wednesdays** they will have English, maths, RE, PE and science. On **Thursdays** they will have English, maths, science, Spanish and history. On **Fridays** they will have English, maths, geography, computing and technology. There will be an assembly between 9.00am and 9.15am every day. Registration is at 8.50am each day. Lesson 1 is 9.15–10.15. Lesson 2 is 10.15–11.15. Lesson 3 is 11.30–12.30. Lunch is 12.30–1.15. Lesson 4 is 1.15–2.15. Lesson 5 is 2.30–3.30. Morning break is 11.15–11.30. Afternoon break is 2.15–2.30.

	Mon	**Tues**	**Wed**	**Thurs**	**Fri**
8.50–9.00					
9.00–9.15					
9.15–10.15					
10.15–11.15					
11.15–11.30					
11.30–12.30					
12.30–1.15					
1.15–2.15					
2.15–2.30					
2.30–3.30					

How did you do?

Structuring with punctuation

Write a sentence containing one colon and one or two commas to describe each of the following pictures.

How did you do?

Using semicolons within a list

Semicolons are used to mark the boundary between two independent clauses, to show a link between two things or to separate complicated items in a list.

Complete the postcard below by adding semicolons in the correct places.

Hi Kelly,

I am having a great time in Ibiza where I have already been to the beach four times stayed up till ten o'clock every night got the beginnings of a monster tan and learned to say 'Please' and 'Thank you' in Spanish.

See you soon,

Tracy

Kelly Dyer

147 Mount Close

Didsworth

Staffordshire

DW12 4RJ

Punctuate this diary entry by adding semicolons in the correct places.

Thursday 22nd January

In English today we had to write a story.

My story was a really scary one in a haunted house with cobwebs hanging from the ceiling doors that creaked and squeaked unexplained thumping noises all the lights going out and lightning striking the chimney.

How did you do?

Link the clauses

We use colons to introduce: lists, summaries, examples, quotations and second clauses that expand or illustrate the first clause.

Use colons and semicolons to punctuate the following sentences.

1. In school today we learned how to say 'Good morning' and 'Good evening' in Spanish how to make a great pizza how to use a thesaurus and how to use colons.

_____

_____

_____

2. Shakespeare wrote The Merchant of Venice, which was about a money-lender Macbeth, which is known as 'the Scottish play' and Hamlet, which is set in Denmark.

_____

_____

_____

3. For this recipe you will need the juice of four oranges the skins of three lemons a litre of water and 200g of sugar.

_____

_____

_____

4. Alligators are reptiles. Other reptiles include saltwater crocodiles Indonesian Komodo dragons and long-nosed chameleons.

_____

_____

_____

How did you do?

Dash, dash, dash

Draw lines to join the parts of the sentences.

Anya has invited all of her friends	— reds, greens and browns.
I have to catch the next bus	— sand doesn't.
Salt dissolves in water	— Charlie, Emma and Asher.
Sian likes pizza	— in addition, she likes curry.
I went to India when I was young	— it leaves at four o'clock.
Autumn has wonderful colours	— so long ago.

Which two other punctuation marks could have been used in some of the sentences instead of the dashes?

_____

Rewrite two of the sentences using the alternative punctuation marks.

_____

_____

_____

How did you do?

Separating clauses

Circle the last word in the first clause and the first word in the second clause in these sentences.

1. There is one thing you need to know about dogs as pets they are hard work.

2. Preston is the county town of Lancashire Matlock is the county town of Derbyshire.

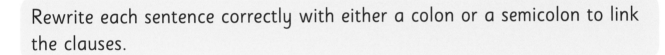

3. Granite is a very hard rock limestone is a softer one.

4. There was only one option he'd have to have fish and chips for dinner.

5. It's my birthday next week I will be eleven.

Rewrite each sentence correctly with either a colon or a semicolon to link the clauses.

1. _____

_____

2. _____

_____

3. _____

_____

4. _____

_____

5. _____

_____

How did you do?

Marking boundaries

Rewrite the following sentences with dashes to mark the boundaries between the clauses.

1. I had chips for tea I really enjoyed them.

_____

2. Anya likes dancing Tamsin enjoys singing.

_____

3. There are three primary colours red, green and blue.

_____

4. Some children walk to school others come on the bus.

_____

Rewrite each of the sentences using either a colon or a semicolon in place of the dashes.

5. I had chips for tea I really enjoyed them.

_____

6. Anya likes dancing Tamsin enjoys singing.

_____

7. There are three primary colours red, green and blue.

_____

8. Some children walk to school others come on the bus.

_____

How did you do?

Practise using colons, semicolons and dashes

Replace the dashes in the following sentences with either colons or semicolons.

1. Mark is good at table tennis – he practises a lot.

_____

2. Yuri can speak four languages – Latvian, English, German and Russian.

_____

3. Final results – most people prefer swimming to running.

_____

4. Practice is the noun – practise is the verb.

_____

5. Donna rides to school – Ronnie walks.

_____

Make up two sentences of your own, one using a colon and one using a semicolon. For each one, explain why you have used the punctuation mark.

6. _____

I have used a colon because: _____

_____

7. _____

I have used a semicolon because: _____

_____

How did you do?

Colons, semicolons and dashes

Insert colons and semicolons in the correct boxes below to complete an article for your school's newsletter.

1. In our class, the favourite colours are ☐ blue, yellow and purple. Quite a few people like red ☐ black is much more unpopular.

2. There were lots of reasons for the choices ☐ yellow and red are cheerful colours ☐ blue is very bright ☐ black is miserable.

3. Our teacher said ☐ "This has been a really good investigation. Thank you all for your opinions."

4. I thought it was really interesting ☐ Claire didn't.

5. We'll be doing another investigation next week ☐ they are great fun.

Insert dashes into the correct places in these sentences.

6. "Thanks for the present it was great."

_____

7. "Honestly, it was no bother no bother at all"

_____

8. "It's my favourite colour green. What's your favourite colour blue?"

_____

9. "Yes, it's blue no wait it's red!"

_____

How did you do?

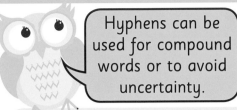

Hyphens can be used for compound words or to avoid uncertainty.

Hyphens

In each of the following examples, one word is missing its hyphen. Circle the words and write them correctly in the boxes.

1. It was so cold last night that we had to deice the car this morning.

2. We have started drinking semiskimmed milk instead of full-fat.

3. It would be selfish if I did not admit to a selfinterest in this.

4. We have had doubleglazed windows put into our house.

5. Here is an extract from an exfootballer's autobiography.

The words below all need hyphens. Write a sentence using each of the words to show its meaning.

| fine tune | mid 1990s | sister in law | top notch |

_____

_____

_____

_____

How did you do?

More hyphens

All of the following sentences are missing a hyphen. Rewrite them, inserting hyphens in the correct places.

1. Sunita is a long standing friend.

_____

2. Police help dog bite victim.

_____

3. In the sports news today, Manchester United's manager has resigned but they have resigned their former striker.

_____

4. The group consisted of ten year old children.

_____

5. He plays in a heavy metal band.

_____

6. Glasshouse, an infamous rock band of the 1990s, has reformed but that does not mean that they are reformed characters.

_____

7. There were seventy odd people at the concert.

_____

8. Cheryl Kane is a little known author.

_____

9. I have a great grandmother.

_____

10. The zoo has opened a small animal room.

_____

How did you do?

What does it really mean?

Rewrite these sentences using hyphens to avoid any ambiguity.

1. I need to recover my sofa.

_____

2. The teacher asked for a remark on some exam papers.

_____

3. In science today, the laughing gas canister exploded!

_____

4. I filled up a hot water bottle.

_____

5. *Thriller*, by Michael Jackson, is apparently the best selling album ever.

_____

6. He went into the changing room cubicle.

_____

7. They all thought the state of the art room was amazing!

_____

8. I resent the letter.

_____

9. I had to reform my model when some parts fell off.

_____

10. Big city traffic is worse than small town traffic.

_____

How did you do?

What do they do?

Circle all of the punctuation marks in this text.

My cousin has seven dogs! They are: three collies, two mongrels, two spaniels and a St Bernard. Where does she keep them? Mostly in her bedroom – I don't know how. She's happy; her mother isn't.

Name each of the punctuation marks in the order they are used in the passage.

_____

_____

_____

Imagine you are a punctuation mark. Write an advertisement to sell yourself to writers. There is an example below for you to follow.

Buy me! I'm a colon and you really need me. I have a stylish shape that looks attractive. Which other punctuation mark has two dots on top of each other? I can make your writing more cohesive and get you the highest marks! People think I only introduce lists but I have many more uses: I can start your summaries and quotations; begin examples and separate clauses from each other. I'm really useful but rare, so buy me while you can!

_____

_____

_____

_____

Find the mistakes

Circle all the punctuation mistakes in this passage.

There were lots of things Harrison did not like about being a spy? the international travel: pretending to be someone else: and the danger. He was used to the danger though it was there all the time. Today was just the same another job. He had got into the building and now he had to get out. He picked up his car keys. his briefcase. his camera; and his false passport,

Harrison opened the window! slid through it! dropped the briefcase to the ground followed it down and ran. Some people would have been scared! he wasn't one of them?

Rewrite the passage using the correct punctuation.

_____

_____

_____

_____

_____

_____

_____

_____

_____

How did you do?

Make it clearer

Look at the sentence below.

I know a girl who has a stick called Jen.

The meaning of the sentence is not clear. Give two possible meanings for it.

_____

_____

We can use punctuation to make the meaning clearer.

For example: I know a girl – who has a stick – called Jen.

Use dashes, commas or brackets to make the meanings of the following sentences clear.

1. My auntie loves cooking her dog and playing tennis.

_____

2. Most of the time travellers worry about being late.

_____

3. "Let's eat Grandma."

_____

4. The girls who had practised enjoyed the event; the boys didn't.

_____

5. She was talking about her gran who has a sister with one eye.

_____

How did you do?

Make it clearer

Use the correct punctuation to give this sentence four completely different meanings.

The way we punctuate affects the way our writing is understood.

An old gentleman called grandpa.

1. _____

This means:

_____

2. _____

This means:

_____

3. _____

This means:

_____

4. _____

This means:

_____

How did you do?

Make it more interesting

Use the verbs in the box to complete the verb table.

amble   dash   rinse   bathe   saunter   survey
race   observe   sprint   stroll   shampoo   view

Verb	Alternatives		
to run			
to walk			
to watch			
to wash			

Write one sentence using one of the alternatives for each verb.

_____

_____

_____

_____

Choose one of your sentences and explain why it is more interesting than it would have been using the original verb.

I think sentence number _____ is more interesting because _____

_____

_____

_____

How did you do?

Make it even more interesting

Use a thesaurus to help you make a verb bank for the following verbs.

Verb	Alternatives		
to annoy			
to wave			
to sleep			
to shout			

Use a thesaurus to help you make an adverb bank for the following adverbs.

Adverb	Alternatives		
very			
proudly			
quickly			
loudly			

Rewrite the following sentences using your alternative adverbs and verbs. For each sentence explain how your word is an improvement on the original.

1. I was very annoyed to miss the bus.

_____

This is an improvement because: _____

_____

2. The victorious athletes waved their flags proudly.

_____

This is an improvement because: _____

_____

How did you do?

Playing with words

Complete this table by writing a definition for each word class and giving two examples.

Word class	Definition	Examples
adjective		
adverb		
conjunction		
noun		
determiner		
preposition		
pronoun		
verb		

Here is an example of a nonsense sentence that uses all of the word classes.

Seven (determiner) hairy (adjective) dinosaurs (noun) juggled (verb) carefully (adverb) behind (preposition) us (pronoun) for (conjunction) two (determiner) long (adjective) hours (noun).

Make up a silly sentence of your own that uses all the word classes. You could use the words from your examples. Don't forget to include the word classes in brackets.

How did you do?

What's missing?

Complete the passages below by inserting words from the box.

Julie _____ quickly towards the old _____. She had

_____ there before _____ never on her own. _____

looked _____ at her _____. Could it really be that

_____?

shed	but	hastily	time
intently	watch	Julie	carefully
stumbled	she	hurried	though
been	churchyard	visited	house

Insert the words you have used in the table below. Then write its word class.

Word	Word class	Word	Word class

Complete this passage by inserting your own words. Write the word class for each word in brackets.

Tariq was _____ (_____). He had not seen his

_____ (_____) for _____ (_____) days.

_____ (_____) wanted to call the police _____ he

was afraid. Finally, he dialled the number and waited _____

(_____) for the response.

How did you do?

Media words

Different types of media use different words.

Write the correct word class next to each word in the boxes below.

Advertising

new _____

best _____

bargain _____

special _____

improved _____

Social media

wiki _____

app _____

blog _____

hashtag _____

text _____

Television news

broadcast _____

correspondent _____

regional _____

Radio

audio _____

jingle _____

soundbite _____

Which word class had the most words?

_____

Which words could belong to more than one word class?

_____

Which word classes are not represented?

_____

How did you do?

What makes it interesting?

Read the following passage. Consider the words in bold and explain how they make the passage interesting. Write the word class for each word in the brackets.

A **bitter** wind **whipped** across Briggs Brothers' Scrapyard. It drove harsh rain **violently** before it, like machine gun bullets. In a distant corner, away from all of the other **mangled** vehicles, Cara the Caravanette **huddled** silently, praying that the storm would soon blow over.

From *Cara the Caravanette* by Graham Fletcher

1. Bitter (word class: _____) makes the passage interesting because:

_____

_____

2. Whipped (word class: _____) makes the passage interesting because:

_____

_____

3. Violently (word class: _____) makes the passage interesting because:

_____

_____

4. Mangled (word class: _____) makes the passage interesting because:

_____

_____

5. Huddled (word class: _____) makes the passage interesting because:

_____

_____

How did you do?

Using prepositions and adverbs

Underline and identify the adverbs and prepositions in the following sentences. The first one has been done for you.

For example: Ajay sensibly locked his bike chain around the wheels and carefully left it against the wall.

Adverbs: <u>sensibly, carefully</u> Prepositions: <u>around, against</u>

1. Erin expertly swerved the white ball around the black to gently push the pink into the middle pocket.

Adverbs: _____ Prepositions: _____

2. The hikers had to tread carefully between the bushes to reach the badly signposted path behind them.

Adverbs: _____ Prepositions: _____

3. We did some unbelievably hard training during our preparation for the marathon we reluctantly did in June.

Adverbs: _____ Prepositions: _____

4. I could hear an amazingly loud scream coming from inside the old hall.

Adverb: _____ Preposition: _____

5. Ralf almost caught the ball but it was beyond his reach.

Adverb: _____ Preposition: _____

6. We were beaten easily despite a late comeback.

Adverb: _____ Preposition: _____

7. I can speak French fast and fluently so I am confident when I go over there.

Adverbs: _____ Preposition: _____

How did you do?

Sentence forms

Name the four different forms of sentences.

1. _____

2. _____

3. _____

4. _____

After each of the following sentences, write its form.

5. You've done that well! _____

6. How did you do that? _____

7. This is the way to do it. _____

8. Do it! _____

Write your own example of each form and write its name next to it.

9. _____

10. _____

11. _____

12. _____

In these sentences the punctuation has been removed. Write the sentence form after each one.

13. Where is it _____

14. It's over there _____

15. That's not where it should be _____

How did you do?

More sentence forms

Draw lines to link each sentence to the correct form.

Argentina is in South America.

That's right!

It's not difficult to find it.

Where is Argentina?

Find out where Argentina is.

Is Argentina near Uruguay?

It's really not difficult!

Look it up in an atlas.

How many people live in Argentina?

Go online to look it up.

That's a huge number!

Over 40 million people live in Argentina.

Exclamation

Question

Statement

Command

Now write a statement, a question, a command and an exclamation about the place in which you live.

_____

_____

_____

How did you do?

Changing sentence forms

The way we structure sentences and the punctuation we use can change their forms.

"Be home by nine o'clock." is a command.
"Be home by nine o'clock?" is a question.
The punctuation tells us how it would sound.

"I'll be home by nine o'clock." is a statement.
"I'll be home by nine o'clock!" is an exclamation.

Rewrite the following sentences to change their forms.

1. I won't be late. (statement)

_____ (exclamation)

2. You won the match! (exclamation)

_____ (question)

3. This is a long bus ride! (exclamation)

_____ (statement)

Sometimes we need to change some of the words to change the sentence form.

"Put your pens down." is a command.
"Could you put your pens down?" is a question.

Rewrite the following sentences to change them from statements to questions.

4. It is Friday. _____

5. You know how to do that. _____

6. You can come for tea. _____

How did you do?

Making different forms of sentences

Write the correct sentence form next to the sentences below.

1. You've done that really well. _____

2. Have you done that really well? _____

3. You've done that really well! _____

4. Do it really well. _____

For each of the sentences, identify the form. Rewrite the sentence in a different form then identify the form of your sentences.

5. Rachel is wearing a red top (form: _____)

_____ (form: _____)

6. Read a book every day (form: _____)

_____ (form: _____)

7. Do cats like fish? (form: _____)

_____ (form: _____)

8. Stop shouting! (form: _____)

_____ (form: _____)

How did you do?

Add to it

Add clauses to the descriptions below, to help make them more interesting. Use the pictures to help you.

Sunitra was not expecting a kite because

_____

_____

Everyone crammed into the family's tiny car. They drove to the park where _____

_____

_____ to the top of hill.

Sunitra flew the kite on top of the hill. The wind was really strong and _____

_____

leaving her with just the string and _____

_____

into the sky then dropped into a tree where

_____

Robbie the dog jumped high _____

_____

Sunitra gave him a hug and _____

How did you do?

Conjunction glue

Use conjunctions to join these sentences.

For example: My mum has a new job. She can now afford a new car.
My mum has a new job so she can now afford a new car.

1. We had to walk home. We hadn't got enough money for the bus.

   _____

2. I had to leave the beach. The tide was coming in quickly.

   _____

3. I washed all of the dishes. My family had finished eating.

   _____

Join these sentences by making relative clauses.

For example: My mum has a new car. It goes like a rocket. _My mum has a new car that goes like a rocket._

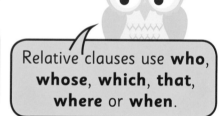

Relative clauses use **who**, **whose**, **which**, **that**, **where** or **when**.

4. I am going to Malta. It is in the Mediterranean Sea.

   _____

5. Josie is a good player. She scores lots of goals.

   _____

6. My uncle has just come back from Blackpool. He went to the top of the Tower.

   _____

7. I sent a postcard from Greece. It arrived in England a week later.

   _____

How did you do?

More is better

Including more detail in your writing will often make it better.

Join these clauses with conjunctions. Avoid using: 'for', 'and', 'nor', 'but', 'or', 'yet' and 'so'.

1. Robin Hood knew that he would have to stay as an outlaw _____ King John was on the throne.

2. King John was in charge for now _____ things would change when his brother, Richard returned from the Crusades.

3. He could go to the cinema _____ he had enough money to pay for it.

4. I checked the bus timetable _____ I went to catch it.

5. She went out without her coat _____ it was raining.

Insert a phrase or clause in each of these sentences.

6. The old building _____ was made safe by the Fire Brigade.

7. The monster moved towards the village where _____ _____.

8. I heard the car's engine, _____, before I saw the car.

9. The rain, _____, poured all night.

10. Tigers, _____, are in danger of extinction.

How did you do?

Joining clauses

You are going to join clauses using conjunctions. In the sentence starter box, write the beginning of a sentence that could be followed by a coordinating conjunction and then complete the sentence.

Sentence starter	
Coordinating conjunction	and
Continuation of sentence	

Use the same sentence starter. This time the link is a subordinating conjunction. Add a new ending to the sentence.

Sentence starter	
Subordinating conjunction	since
Continuation of sentence	

Repeat the process again, but this time the link is a subordinating conjunction that will create a relative clause after it.

Sentence starter	
Subordinating conjunction	when
Continuation of sentence	

How did you do?

Make your writing really detailed

Use one of the adjectives below and another one of your own to build up an expanded noun phrase about a creepy castle.

(eerie) (mysterious) (unwelcoming) (menacing) (mottled)

I crept towards the _____ castle.

Now choose a modifying noun to give more information about the castle.

(stone) (granite) (timber) (brick) (concrete)

Where will your modifying noun fit into your sentence?

I crept towards the _____ castle.

Finally, add some more detail using a preposition phrase at the end of the sentence.

(at the top of the hill) (in the moonlight) (on the other side of the moat)

I crept towards the _____ castle _____.

Make up your own similar sentences using these expanded noun phrases and write them below.

1. the deep mine _____

2. the dry desert _____

3. the dangerous planet _____

4. the cold sea _____

How did you do? ✔ ?

Progress chart

Tick (✔) Ollie when you have completed the chapter.

1 Verbs and tenses

2 Formal and informal speech and writing

3 Complexities in sentences

6 Getting to grips with grammar

5 Punctuation

4 Cohesion, organisation and presentation

Well done! You have now completed the Grammar and punctuation workbook for ages 10–11.